What Happened to our MONEY?

An introductory
financial guide
for young couples

Gary Miller

PUBLISHER'S ACKNOWLEDGMENT

The Stewardship Education Fund at Anabaptist Foundation funded the development of this book. To learn more about their work, or to order additional copies of this book, call 800-653-9817 or write to Anabaptist Foundation, 1245 Old Route 15, New Columbia, PA 17856.

TABLE OF CONTENTS

INTRODUCTION

Ignorance of money management and the meaning of money often sets young people on a path of financial hardship, resulting in anxiety, marital discord, depression, and envy.

People in financial stress often believe more money would solve their woes. But while money is necessary, our personal character and habits are just as important. There are numerous stories of people who earned hundreds of thousands of dollars a year, yet upon losing their job, could not survive for half a year on their assets. Usually, our main problem is not an insufficient income; it is our own laziness, ignorance, or short-sighted perspective.

This book presents us with a foundational truth on which to build our financial lives: "The earth is the Lord's . . ." (Psalm 24:1).

God owns everything. At the same time, He has made us stewards of His goods. As stewards responsible to God for our use of His resources, our top priority is to glorify Him and build His

Kingdom. We are accountable to God in *all* things.

In this book, Gary Miller explains how to track your income and expenses, prioritize your spending according to Kingdom values, and live within the constraints of your income and priorities. You will be inspired to focus on serving God and others first, leaving your financial future in God's hands.

Whether you are rich or poor, the principles here can free you from an obsession with money and set you on a path to financial competence and contentment.

—Elmer Stoltzfus
Leola, Pennsylvania

Chapter 1

WHAT HAPPENED TO OUR MONEY?

A mos[1] ripped the overdraft statement from the envelope, glanced at it, and crumpled it in his fist. "This has got to stop," he growled as he stalked back to the house from the mailbox. Yanking open the back door, he shouted, "Mandy! I'm tired of these bank overdrafts! Why do you keep spending all our money on stuff we don't need? Now you wrote a check for $65 at the fabric store when there was nothing in the account. You've got to quit spending money!"

"Don't talk to me

---

[1] Amos and Mandy are an imaginary couple.

about spending money," Mandy snapped. "We would've had plenty, but you just *had* to buy that new rifle last month! And it might help if you balanced the checkbook sometimes, like other men do. How am *I* supposed to know how much is in there?" She turned and left the room.

Amos flopped into a chair and un-crumpled the overdraft statement, smarting from Mandy's parting shot. He was weary of bickering over money all the time. A year ago, when they had married, life had seemed so simple. With a good job at a local construction company, Amos earned at least as much as other young couples in their community. Yet here they were, out of money again. With Mandy expecting a baby and their finances constantly out of control, the future was starting to look scary.

Amos looked out the window, thinking. Almost every month they faced some kind of financial problem. Why did they always have trouble with money? Did every young couple struggle like this?

Usually, the only time Amos and Mandy talked about money was when there wasn't enough of it, but now Amos wondered if they should be paying more attention to their finances. How could they afford to have children? They had already borrowed from Mandy's parents, and they had nothing saved for the future. How would they ever purchase their own home?

The Problem

Many young couples start out like Amos and Mandy. The husband gets a job, the wife manages the affairs at home, and they don't begin talking about finances until they have a problem. They buy the things their friends are buying and do the things their friends are doing, yet they have never really discussed long-term goals for their family.

> *Many young couples don't begin talking about finances until they have a problem.*

Imagine a carpenter trying to build a house this way—he brings the lumber to the building site, cuts boards to shorter lengths, and starts nailing them together. He doesn't have a set of plans, but he has observed other carpenters doing these things, so he assumes if he goes through the same motions, a nice house will emerge. What kind of structure would this carpenter build? It would be a mess, wouldn't it?

We all understand that you cannot build a house without a plan of some kind, yet we easily forget that this same principle applies to our finances. Life is full of choices. We walk into a store or open a catalog and see many things we would like to have. How can we decide which items to purchase? How do we know what we can afford? If there is enough money in our checking account, does that mean we can buy something? If others are buying these things, does that mean we should too? We obviously need a plan to guide us through our many financial decisions, but how can we create such a plan? What reference points should we use?

The Bible has much to say about money and possessions. Within it we find teaching on ownership, sharing with others, and planning for the future. It contains powerful warnings regarding debt and accumulating earthly wealth. It teaches us the importance of a good work ethic and how to relate to our employers. As followers of the Lord Jesus, we need to look closely at what He has to say on this topic.

Maybe you are just starting out on your own and have never given much thought to money; or maybe, like Amos and Mandy, you are having financial difficulties now. Whatever your situation, God has a plan for your home, and His Word can guide you in working through everyday financial decisions and developing a Kingdom-focused vision.

Chapter 2

DEVELOPING A VISION

As the evening darkness gathered, Amos knew he needed to apologize to Mandy for his angry outburst. Their lack of money wasn't her fault any more than his, and as the head of the home, he was mainly responsible for their lack of planning.

Amos was soberly facing reality. He and Mandy had married, rented a house, and would soon have a child to support. Yet they had given little thought to their finances—they were just doing what many others in their community did. Amos was a serious-minded young Christian, and he wanted to do what was right, but now he was perplexed. If he wanted to develop a vision for their home and finances, to whom would he go for advice? Who could he really trust to help him find Biblical direction for his home?

Perhaps he should ask his father—but his father

had always struggled to pay his own bills, so going to him for financial advice didn't seem wise. On the other hand, Amos could think of men in his church who were successful businessmen. Yet sometimes it seemed they were as money-hungry as unbelievers. These men were wealthy and could buy whatever they wanted, but something seemed wrong about their continual pursuit of more wealth. Shouldn't followers of Jesus view money and possessions differently from unbelievers?

Perhaps there was something in the Bible that could help him get a vision for his finances, Amos thought.

That night was a turning point in Amos and Mandy's home. As they began to search the Scriptures together, they found that God has provided a tremendous amount of teaching and direction on this subject. Let's look at some basic truths they found in the Bible about money and possessions.

God Owns Everything

In Psalm 50, the Lord says, ". . . the world is mine, and the fulness thereof." God is the ultimate owner of everything, and we are simply stewards, or managers, of His property. Of course, all of us say we believe this. We understand that God made the world and therefore everything belongs to Him. Yet often our attitude toward potential loss of these possessions shows something different. If these things are not really ours anyway, why do we worry so much about theft or damage to "our" possessions? Why are we so concerned if another brother has more than we do? Maybe we need to be reminded occasionally that these things are not really ours.

God Wants Diligent Stewards

Even before the Fall, God told Adam to "dress and keep"[1] the Garden of Eden. Adam was to be a diligent steward of the garden. This concept is still true today. Even though the world belongs to God, we are responsible for the things He has placed in our care. Someday we will give an account to God for how we use the money, time, and abilities He has entrusted to us. This sober reality should influence how we use these things. If God has given you a sound mind and a strong body, He wants you to use them productively.

---

[1] Genesis 2:15

Debt Is Dangerous

A wise man said many years ago, "The rich ruleth over the poor, and the borrower is servant to the lender."[2] When we decide to follow Jesus, He becomes our master; but this verse says our lender is our master as well. Debt can create a dilemma for the Christian. His loyalty can suddenly become divided.

Being in debt can affect how we read Jesus' teachings. Imagine yourself reading the Bible and suddenly becoming convicted that you should give to a person in need. However, you also know you should be paying off your debt. Should you give money to someone else while you are still in debt? This is an important question to consider, and it shows how debt changes the way you respond to promptings from God's Word.

Borrowing may sometimes be necessary, but we should have a long-term goal to be free from debt. We do not want anything to hinder a proper response to the words of Jesus.

Contentment Is Wealth

The Apostle Paul told Timothy, "And having food and raiment let us be therewith content."[3] Many

---

[2] Proverbs 22:7

[3] 1 Timothy 6:8

young couples find themselves in financial difficulties as a result of ignoring this teaching. Our culture tells us a successful person is someone who is constantly purchasing more things. We are expected to constantly chase bigger, better, faster, and nicer things. However, the Bible teaches a different reality: the wealthiest man is the one who is content with what he has.

> *The wealthiest man is the one who is content with what he has.*

God Comes First

Jesus told His followers, "But seek ye first the kingdom of God, and his righteousness; and all these things shall be added unto you."[4] Yet how often we find ourselves doing just the opposite! We lavish our time and energy on the pursuit of material things, trying to "get ahead," while God and His Kingdom take a lower priority.

God does not take pleasure in seeing us struggle or live in material poverty. However, He does want us to make serving and seeking Him our primary goal. As we seek to obey God, we will

---

[4] Matthew 6:33

find His promises are true. Those who seek God first and follow His instruction to be diligent, trustworthy, honest, and faithful in their work will find God—and they will also find provision for their material needs.

Chapter 3

THE IMPORTANCE OF USING A BUDGET

Most of us tend to believe our greatest financial need is more income. We imagine that if we just had more money, everything would be fine. Amos and Mandy were no different. If Amos's paycheck were just a little larger, they thought, everything would be fine. However, when Amos did get an occasional raise, it never seemed to help. Noticing this, Amos and Mandy began to examine their checkbook. They started tracking past expenses and became keenly aware that their greatest need was *not* more money. What they really needed was a *plan*.

Most people who struggle financially are much like Amos and Mandy. What they need most are worthwhile long-term goals and a plan for reaching them.

Analyzing Our Vision

Each of us has a vision that motivates us. This vision drives our financial decision-making, causing us to buy certain things and avoid others. It is important to be honest about this overriding vision. Maybe you are like Amos and Mandy: you want to be accepted in your community, so you simply imitate what you see others your age doing. Or maybe you are driven by a desire to be thought of as financially successful, so you tend to buy things that make it look as if you are doing well.

Spend some time analyzing the vision driving your choices. Is it really an intense desire to follow Jesus? Have you surrendered your financial life to Jesus Christ? Are you really using the Bible as your primary reference point? It is vitally important to relinquish ownership to God before beginning to develop a financial plan.

Creating a Budget

A budget is like a road map. Both documents

show you how to get from where you are to where you want to be. So start your budget by writing down where you believe God is calling you to go. This might include paying off debt, saving to buy a home, or giving more. Once you have determined where God wants you to go, you need to find out where you are. This is done by tracking past spending. Next, you need a plan to get from where you are to where you want to be. This is the purpose of a budget.

A budget, like a road map, will not produce miracles or money, but it will provide a pathway from where you are to where you want to go. There are many different budgets available, and it is important to find one that fits your needs. If a budget becomes difficult or cumbersome, you will stop using it after a few months.

Many young couples think they don't need a budget or don't have time for the process. Remember, while it is true that budgeting will take some effort, the cost of going through life without a plan can be very high. Failing to plan is planning to fail. To reach worthwhile

> *Failing to plan is planning to fail.*

financial goals, you need to plan. Someone has said, "If you don't care where you are going, any old road will work." The opposite is also true: if you have a definite destination, choosing the right road is very important.

Uniting on Vision

If you are married, it is essential that you and your spouse are united as you face financial issues. When couples experience stress over finances, money is rarely the real problem. Rather, couples argue over money because they have not united on a vision for their home. It is vital that couples pray together, search the Word of God together, and commit their home to the service of God. Uniting on a Kingdom vision will eliminate many disagreements over how money should be spent.

Staying on Track

Regardless of how well-thought-out your budget is, you will have difficulties. As these challenges come, keep going back to your overriding vision for your home. In light of your vision to save for a new home or share more with others, should you really be buying that new rifle or more knick-knacks to decorate your home? Such issues can be challenging to work through, but if you are serious about reaching your goals and keeping your budget on track, open communication in your marriage is essential.

Chapter 4

THE POWER OF FREQUENT TRANSACTIONS

As Amos and Mandy began to work through their financial difficulties, each secretly suspected the other was most at fault. They decided to begin tracking their expenses. Daily they wrote down the cost of everything they purchased. At the end of each month they totaled all the expenses into separate categories to determine where their money was going.

Tracking their expenses proved to be revealing! For example, Amos had a habit of purchasing a Coke and a bag of potato chips every day at break time. This seemed insignificant, at a cost of only $3 per day. But as they began adding up their monthly expenses, Amos realized his snack cost $60 a month. Even more astounding, this added up to $720 a year. Suddenly his little snack took on a different appearance. If he continued this habit, he would spend $3600 in five years—a good percentage of what he needed for a down payment on a house!

The revelation of Amos's weakness provided  little satisfaction for Mandy, however, for she learned something about herself as well. She began to realize that the quick and easy prepared meals she had been buying came with a price. Shocked and embarrassed at how much this convenience cost weekly, Mandy began to comprehend why her mother had raised her own produce, canned as much as possible, and seldom purchased ready-made products.

Tracking expenses taught Amos and Mandy that frequent transactions have a high cost. It is one thing to purchase a soft drink at an auction once a month; it is entirely another when this becomes a daily habit. When small purchases become frequent, they can derail your long-term financial plans.

The Blessing of Frequent Transactions

Although frequent small transactions can cost you dearly over time, the reverse is also true. You can use the power of frequent transactions to your advantage. Suppose you have a long-term goal of saving for a down payment on a house. Setting aside $30 each week may sound insignificant and hardly worth your time, but if you do this over a period of five years, you will save $7800.

> *The primary lack is not money but wise management.*

Often we fail to achieve meaningful goals, not because we lack money, but because we spend too much on smaller, unnecessary items. The primary lack is not money but wise management. Proverbs says, "He that loveth pleasure shall be a poor man . . . "[1] The person who habitually makes decisions based on what feels good at the moment will experience constant financial difficulty.

Many young couples today believe if they just

---

[1] Proverbs 21:17

had more cash, their troubles would be over. The truth is that most couples already have sufficient income but fail to understand the power of frequent financial transactions.

Chapter 5

GOD'S DELIVERYMEN

Choosing to live out Biblical truth will always bring change to our lives. Amos and Mandy discovered this as they began praying for a God-honoring vision, seeking His will in their choices, and communicating openly with each other. Something amazing began to occur: they found extra money in their checkbook!

Now Amos and Mandy were faced with a new question: What should they do with the extra money? One evening as they were reading their Bible together, they came across an interesting verse in the book of Ephesians. The message was simple, but it had a deep effect on Amos and Mandy's lives. This verse says that a man of God will be law-abiding and diligent, and it concludes by telling why. It says he is to work so that "he may have to give to him that needeth."[1]

Both Amos and Mandy had grown up knowing that hard work was a Biblical concept. They had assumed that the purpose of work was to provide for one's own family. But this verse told them something else. It said a healthy, hardworking man should also labor with the intent of blessing others.

God intends that we work diligently, having a goal to pass on some of the resulting income to those in need. There will always be people who cannot support themselves. Jesus said, "Ye have the poor always with you . . ."[2] God intends that those who can earn an income provide for the needs of those who cannot.

As stewards, we become God's deliverymen. Most of us are familiar with having a UPS man come to our home. It is his job to deliver packages,

 some of which contain valuable items. However, the value of the items is of little concern to the UPS man. His job is

---

[1] Ephesians 4:28

[2] Matthew 26:11

simply to deliver the packages safely.

What would happen to a UPS deliveryman who began taking some packages home instead of delivering them? He wouldn't keep his job very long, would he?

Called to Deliver God's Goods

As God's "deliverymen," we find ourselves in a similar place. God gives us resources, intending that we share with those in need. But sometimes we take our eyes off God's intent and begin imagining how these valuable assets could make our own lives more pleasant. Perhaps another couple in our community buys some new home furnishings, and although we know the furniture we have is fine, we feel pressure to upgrade. Instead of passing on the extra resources God has placed in our hands for delivery, we are tempted to use more than we really need.

In the Old Testament, God required the children of Israel to return 10 percent of their increase back to the Lord.[3] This is referred to as *tithing*, and the amount was a requirement under the Mosaic Law. However, in addition to regular, mandatory giving, God also provided opportunities for people

---

[3] Leviticus 27:30

to show their thankfulness by giving away their possessions voluntarily.[4]

Tithing was very important in the Old Testament, but today God is calling us to something much higher than just giving a percentage. When God owns a man, He must control everything that man owns.

> **When God owns a man, He must control everything that man owns.**

We see examples of this in the book of Acts. The record shows early believers voluntarily giving up everything they owned and cheerfully sharing with others.[5] These Christians understood the great price Jesus had paid for them on the cross, and they understood that the only proper response was to relinquish ownership of their material goods.

Regular Giving

It is important to establish regular, consistent giving. God has given us much both naturally and spiritually, and we should share regularly with

---

[4] Leviticus 22:18–23, Numbers 15:3, Deuteronomy 12:6, 17

[5] Acts 2:44–47, Acts 4:33–37

those in need. God required 10 percent in the past, and this may still be a good place to start. When we do not have a consistent plan, we easily forget to give.

It is also important to watch for ways to share spontaneously. I don't think the Good Samaritan had planned to care for the man he found lying on the road, half dead.[6] The Samaritan may have been a regular giver, yet that did not excuse him from helping this man in need. He was watching for extra opportunities to help others, and this should be our goal as well.

---

[6] Luke 10:25–37

Chapter 6

SEASONS OF LIFE

A mos and Mandy are young, and their future is unknown. They don't have much extra money now, but what if they live until they are eighty-five years old? What kind of changes might those years bring to their finances? Based on the changes in other American families, let's see what this might look like on a graph.

As you look at the graph on the next page, try to ignore the actual numbers. This graph is simply to help us get a picture of discretionary income and gain a vision for its proper use. The upper line on the graph (the top boundary of the dark area) represents the income Amos brought home, and the lower line (the top boundary of the lower lighter area) represents the expenses required to operate their home.

As you can see by looking at the graph, Amos had

Discretionary Income

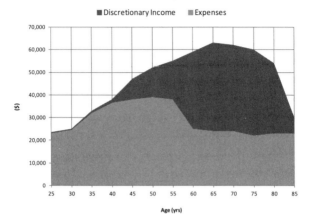

an annual wage of $22,000 at the age of twenty-five. Over the years his income climbed as his employer appreciated his faithfulness and gradually increased his wages. By the time Amos was forty-five, his income had grown to about $46,000 per year. At the age of sixty-five, Amos's income peaked at $63,000, then slowly began to decrease as his declining health kept him from working as many hours. Finally, Amos died when he was eighty-five years old.

Lifetime Expenses and Discretionary Income

As you can see from the graph, Amos's expenses also changed over the years. Those first few years were pretty tough. After all the necessary expenses, not much money was left over. Let's assume Amos and Mandy borrowed money and purchased an older farmhouse that needed some repairs. Over the next ten years they had six children, which brought additional expenses. The year Amos turned fifty-five, their mortgage was finally paid off, and this had a great impact on their budget.

You can see on the graph that for the first time in their married life, Amos and Mandy's expenses began to fall. With the house paid off and the children beginning to leave home, their expenses continued to fall. During the last ten years of Amos's life, their expenses remained relatively stable each year until he died.

Now, let's leave the expenses and income and look at the area between the two. This area, which is dark on the graph, represents discretionary income throughout Amos and Mandy's life. This is the money that flowed through their hands and was not needed for survival.

Seasons of Life

One lesson we can learn from this graph is that our lives have seasons. Many young families wish they could give more. We should all be giving to those in need, yet during these early years, we may not have much extra to share. These are the years, however, when our vision is being formed.

Early Years—Develop the Vision
Look over the graph of Amos's life again and notice the years between twenty-five and thirty-five. You will notice there is little discretionary income during those years. While most young families have little to give during this season of life, something of profound importance is occurring. During this time, couples develop longings, and the direction those longings lean will greatly influence the rest of their lives.

Suppose that during the first ten years of their married life, Amos and Mandy focused on society and the affluence that surrounded them. Even though they could not afford extra things, they began to long for them. Conversations in their home might have sounded like this: "I wish we could redecorate our bathroom. Did you see how nice Mary's looks since they remodeled?"

> *Discretionary money always follows our longings.*

Discretionary money always follows our longings. If Amos and Mandy had longings like this during their early years, what will happen to their extra money when the mortgage is finally paid off? Obviously, the money that had been going to the mortgage will begin flowing toward the things they had longed for.

But suppose they had learned to view life with a Kingdom perspective, seeing themselves as stewards. In the early years they might have said, "I just heard that Sarah is having medical problems again. I wish we had enough money to help her." Or, "I read that there is a desperate need for Bibles in some countries where Christians are persecuted. I wish we could find a way to help." Again, money eventually follows our longings. When Amos and Mandy are able to share more, they will gladly direct their spare dollars toward the needs of others.

The Middle Years

This period of life, also known as *the burden-carrying years*, is a busy time. There are challenges with raising older children, dealing with schooling, teaching children a good work ethic, and perhaps paying off a mortgage. These are usually years of tremendous activity, but as children finally leave the home, more discretionary income is available. During this time, your children are learning by observation what your real priorities are, and as more money becomes available, they will be watching how you use it. They should see that your choices grow out of your love for the Lord and His people.

Latter Years of Opportunity

As you look at the graph of Amos and Mandy's life, it is obvious that most of their discretionary income was available to them between the ages of fifty and seventy. This is true in many homes in America. These years are a rewarding time of blessing and opportunity, a time to pour resources into the Kingdom of God. However, it is also possible to waste these years by squandering discretionary income on leisure, hobbies, and travel for pleasure. What you do with these years will largely depend on the longings you have developed.

Conclusion

As you consider the seasons of your life, use the graph on page 30 to get a vision for using the resources God has placed in your care for the

Kingdom of God. Rather than always longing for the next season, commit to blessing the Kingdom of God wherever you are on the timeline.

Chapter 7

SAVING FOR FUTURE NEED

"I wish this foot would heal!" Amos groaned as he examined his wound. "Our budget is too tight for this. I'm glad we had some money budgeted for savings, but it's almost gone now!" Amos had stepped on a rusty nail two weeks ago. He had tried to take care of it himself, but the foot had become infected and required a doctor's attention anyway. At his last checkup, the doctor had told him he needed to stay home from work a little longer.

Even though you may not be able to think of

any future financial problems, rest assured, they will come. It may be a medical bill, an increase in rent, or the replacement of a piece of machinery. Unexpected expenses are part of life, and you need to be prepared to deal with them. Couples who do not plan for the unforeseen usually end up turning to credit cards or some other type of consumer debt. While some expenses are unknown, there are some we can easily plan for.

Saving for the Known

I had been self-employed for only a year when I received a call that turned my plans upside down. I had been told it was important to save for income tax, but I had not taken that counsel seriously. At the end of the year, when my accountant informed me how much tax I owed, I was shocked!

I had been putting a little money into savings each month, but I had great plans for those funds. Suddenly, all the money I had saved was needed for taxes. I was devastated! I had taken comfort in my growing savings and had spent money on unnecessary things, assuming we were in good shape. Now it was all gone. I began to wonder whether I liked being in business for myself after all. However, I knew it was my own fault. I had failed to plan.

Some future expenses like this are *known needs*. Property taxes, tools, tool replacement—all these expenses will come, and we create financial chaos in our lives if we fail to save for them. Preparing for the future is one of the lessons the Bible tells us we should learn from the ant.[1] God has given the little ant a natural instinct to save food in the summer. It does this because winter is coming. God wants us to learn from that natural instinct. When there is a known need ahead, do not neglect this lesson from the ant.

Saving for the Unknown

In addition to known expenses, there are other expenses, like Amos's foot injury, that are unforeseen. How much should we save for all the things that *might* happen? We must understand that there is no way to save enough for all the unknowns in life. This is why Jesus told us not to lay up treasures on earth.[2] God wants us to trust Him with the unknown. He wants us to understand that He cares for us just as He does for the lilies of the field.

I believe we should have some money set aside for emergencies, but we must be very careful with this. As our savings grow, so will our tendency to begin trusting material wealth rather than God. Jesus said,

---

[1] Proverbs 6:6–8

[2] Matthew 6:19–34

"For where your treasure is, there will your heart be also."[3] This means your heart and your treasure will always be in the same location. As you amass earthly wealth, you will automatically find your heart going there.

How much should we save for the unknown? With all the warnings Jesus gave against hoarding and trusting in earthly wealth, I believe this is a question we should consider prayerfully. For married couples, the husband and wife should consider this question together.

Safe Savings

It is important to note that although Jesus gave warnings about laying up treasures on earth, He is not opposed to storing and accumulation; in fact, He encourages it! However, He is deeply concerned about the *location* of the goods we are accumulating. Jesus said, "Give alms; provide yourselves bags which wax not old, a treasure in the heavens that faileth not, where no thief approacheth, neither moth corrupteth."[4]

This verse says that when you give to the poor in the name of Jesus, you are placing that money in

---

[3] Matthew 6:21

[4] Luke 12:33

the safest place possible. God not only wants you to store wealth; He has also prepared a safe place where it can be preserved!

Chapter 8

THE SNARE OF CONSUMER DEBT

"NO PAYMENTS FOR 6 MONTHS!" proclaimed the advertisement.

"Amos, look at this! We could get that new sofa for the living room now, and we wouldn't have to pay anything for six months!"

Mandy had mentioned new furniture before. Every time she saw that one of their friends had upgraded a piece of furniture, she reexamined their own. It was amazing how fast their sofa had lost its beauty—and the more she looked at advertisements, the worse their furniture looked.

Amos said their finances were too tight to buy furniture. They were still recovering from his medical bills, and spending money on a sofa was not an option. Yet, with no payments for six months, maybe it was time to upgrade!

Buy now and pay later! This system has become

so normal in America that many think nothing of it. But whether we are buying a sofa now and paying later, or using credit cards to pay for something right now, this method rarely works out as expected. Buying household goods on credit is known as consumer debt, and many young couples find themselves unexpectedly entangled in it. What causes people to become ensnared by consumer debt?

The Illusion of Wealth

I remember the day I received my first credit card. Opening the envelope, I read that I had a $2,000 credit limit. I could go into almost any store and walk out with up to $2,000 worth of merchandise. I suddenly felt rich! My mind instantly wandered to all the things that were now within reach. Had anything really changed in my financial status? No, I didn't actually have any more money than before, but consumer debt had given me an illusion of wealth.

Illusions About Tomorrow

Many young couples feel strapped financially due to some

unexpected expense. For some reason—maybe because of medical bills like Amos's—things are a little tight this month. However, they can't see any financial difficulties ahead. The answer seems obvious: get the item now and pay for it later when more money is available.

We like instant gratification, and we are sure the future will be better. This is why many find themselves drowning in consumer debt. Every month will bring its own unexpected expenses, and once you fall into the habit of using consumer debt, you will find yourself on a slippery slope. You will find your mailbox full of interest charges, late fees, and even "better" offers from other consumer debt companies offering to relieve your current struggle—over time.

Understand the Real Problem

What can you do if you find yourself ensnared by consumer debt? First you need to identify the real problem. It is tempting to focus your anger at the financial institutions that charge ridiculous rates and fees. However, if I am impatient and choose to use consumer debt to get an item immediately instead of saving for it, the real problem isn't the credit card company; it is my own spending habits. We prefer to blame others, but we need to understand that getting involved was *our* choice.

Stop Borrowing

You can't dig yourself out of a hole, and you will not recover from consumer debt by continuing to use it. You may need to find someone to hold you accountable in this, but you must stop ignoring reality. You cannot borrow your way out of debt.

Develop a Plan

When you sense you have a problem, start by making a list of all your debts. Total it up and be honest about it. Then *communicate* with your creditors. If you are not able to make a payment, be sure to let them know immediately. As a follower of Jesus, it is important that you leave a clear testimony with your lenders. You will also find them much easier to work with if you communicate.

Sometimes it is good to begin by paying off your smallest debts first. As you pay off one, take the monthly amount you had been paying and start applying it to

> **Recovering from consumer debt is not easy, but it is possible.**

the next one. Paying off debt can provide some much-needed hope as you continue toward your goal of becoming debt-free. Remember, recovering from consumer debt is not easy, but it is possible.

Avoid the Snare

In your struggle for freedom from consumer debt, perhaps the most important key is a long-term vision for living debt-free. Almost always, we fall into consumer debt due to discontentment. We are trying to keep up with others, and we fail to be thankful for what we already have.

The Apostle Paul told Timothy, "But godliness with contentment is great gain."[1] This is still just as true as it was many years ago when it was written. Instead of focusing on accumulating more material things, pour your energy into serving the Lord and blessing the Kingdom of God. Not only will you avoid consumer debt, but you will also find peace in knowing you are living as a faithful steward.

---

[1] 1 Timothy 6:6

Chapter 9

A PLACE OF OUR OWN

Several years passed, and Amos and Mandy continued to read the Scriptures, challenging each other with the teachings of Jesus and trying to apply His words to their daily lives. They still found themselves influenced by peer pressure, and at times it was hard to know which direction to go. They wanted to be faithful followers of Jesus, yet they also wanted to be accepted and admired by their friends. In the conflict between these two desires, the battle was strongest in decisions regarding housing.

Several young couples in their church had recently purchased nice houses built on several acres, tastefully furnished and well landscaped. As Amos and Mandy returned home from visiting these friends, they couldn't help but compare their old rental house to their friends' new homes. When their friends came to visit, Amos and Mandy found themselves secretly embarrassed.

A Place of Our Own

While neither of them talked about their dissatisfaction, the feelings continued to build. One evening as the winter wind whistled outside, banging a loose piece of siding against the house, Mandy sighed. "I wish we could have a place of our own! Imagine how nice it would be to have a house with plenty of room and where we didn't have to worry about what our friends thought."

Amos looked up in surprise. He had been having those same thoughts, but he had no idea Mandy was also discontent. "Maybe it's time for us to think about buying a property," he said. "That new house on the corner is for sale. It looks well-built, and it might be just right for us. Maybe we should see how much they are asking for it. It does seem like we're throwing away a lot of money on rent."

Amos knew there are many good reasons to own your own place. In fact, they had already saved $20,000 toward that goal. *Why keep paying rent year after year,* Amos thought, *when we could use that money to pay off a mortgage?*

The next day Amos called the realtor to

investigate the house on the corner. The realtor was extremely friendly and encouraged Amos and Mandy to wander from room to room, imagining themselves living there. There was no question in their minds—this was exactly what they were looking for! It was beautiful, with plenty of room for children to play, large bedrooms, and a kitchen trimmed in hickory. The property even had a small shop for Amos to work in. Since the owner was eager to sell, the price had been reduced to $200,000.

The realtor assured Amos and Mandy that even with only $20,000 for a down payment, they would qualify for a loan. Excited, they returned home that evening to think about this opportunity.

As they discussed the situation, there was no question that this home would fit their needs. Yet buying it with such a small down payment would

really affect their budget. Due to the condition of their current rental house, their rent was cheap, and the payment on a $180,000 mortgage would be more than double their current rent payment. Where would this additional money come from?

Amos and Mandy went back over their budget, looking for areas where they could reduce their spending. Still imagining themselves in the new house, they began chopping costs from the budget here and there. No sacrifice was too great to gain this new goal of having a place of their own. Amos thought he could put in more hours at work, and Mandy agreed to reduce their food costs.

Is This the Right Path?
"It will be tight," said Mandy, "but I think we could do it."

"Yes, I think we could," Amos said. "But is this really the best path? Remember, we discussed earlier that we wanted to keep our lives as free of debt as possible so we could help others. It would be nice to have that house now, but perhaps we should wait until we have a larger down payment. This is a 30-year loan, and with all the interest, we would end up paying over twice the sale price."

"Maybe you're right, Amos."

Suddenly Mandy's brow cleared as she had a new thought. "Just by going back over our budget, we discovered some new ways we could reduce our expenses. What if we went ahead and made those changes and then put all the extra in savings instead of making a mortgage payment each month? Imagine how fast that would add up!"

Grabbing his calculator, Amos quickly added up the extra they would pay for housing if they purchased this home. When he included the property taxes and potential repairs that come with home ownership, he sat back in his chair and gave a low whistle of amazement.

"By renting a little longer and avoiding those extra costs, it wouldn't take many years until we'd have a much bigger down payment. And look how much that would reduce our mortgage payments!" he exclaimed. As Amos and Mandy considered this path, their excitement grew.

Amos and Mandy wanted a home that would bless God and others, and they suspected that high monthly payments might keep them from this goal. Amos wanted to be free to go help others rebuild after a disaster or take time to assist those in their own community who were struggling. If they always felt strapped financially, would he be able to take off work to serve someone in need? Should they give up all this, just to own a beautiful house?

Amos and Mandy eventually decided not to purchase the house on the corner, not because it wasn't beautiful or wouldn't fill their needs, but because they had grasped a more compelling vision! To buy this house now, they realized, was far too costly. Although it was hard to give up

> *They had grasped a more compelling vision!*

that beautiful house, they realized it simply did not fit into their overriding vision for their family.

After continuing to save for several more years, Amos and Mandy found an older house that needed some work. They took out a small loan, put a lot of work into it, and eventually ended up with a place of their own.

Chapter 10

TEACHING CHILDREN STEWARDSHIP

Amos and Mandy were surprised how much financial teaching the Bible contains. They wondered why they had learned so little about this topic, even though they had grown up in Christian homes. Their church didn't seem to be offering much practical teaching on finances either.

With their second child on the way, Amos and Mandy began to consider what kind of teaching they should provide for their children. How could they encourage their children to seek first the Kingdom of God?[1] How could they impress upon young minds the importance of using their material resources to bless God's Kingdom?

Children Will Be Shaped

Understand that your children's minds *will* be shaped

---

[1] Matthew 6:33

by someone or something. Jesus said, "A man's life consisteth not in the abundance of the things which he possesseth,"[2] yet most people around us believe owning possessions is very important. These two positions are totally opposite. If you don't want your children to absorb the teaching of our culture, you will need to teach them something different.

Our culture shapes us through the advertisements we read, the comments we hear, and the choices we see others make. Let's look at some ways we can teach our children at different ages.

Childhood Through Adolescence

During childhood and adolescence, children have little income and even less expense, yet they are forming important patterns of life. This is a good time to communicate about the importance of saving toward long-term goals. Ask them questions like the following: "What happens when a man doesn't save toward buying a house?" or, "Why do

---

[2] Luke 12:15

you think people get in trouble with credit cards? How could this be avoided?" Questions like these can lead to good discussions that will help prepare children for the future.

> *Children need to leave a store with money they chose not to spend.*

It is important that children learn self-control and financial restraint. They need to learn how to leave a store with money they chose not to spend because they are saving it for something more important. To do this, they will need some money of their own. As a parent, you will need to give thought and prayer to this.

Children should be taught the importance of regular giving. Many of us in America have more than we need, and children need to learn to look at life from the perspective of global reality. Tell them about living conditions in other parts of the world. Allow them to experience the joy that comes from choosing to share with the needy.

Teenage Years

During these years, young people's income and

expenses may increase. They begin to experience new freedoms, responsibilities, and opportunities to bless others. At the same time, they face increasing peer pressure. This is a good time to teach them how to focus on a long-term goal, the importance of budgeting, and how to avoid being swayed by others' choices.

Do they know how much money it takes to purchase a home? What about buying tools for work or starting a new business? Do they understand how to save for these major expenses? These topics provide wonderful opportunities for healthy discussions with teenagers.

One of the hardest things for parents to do is to watch their children make poor choices. Yet it is essential that we allow young people to learn. I remember making some very poor investments in my older teenage years, some of which cost me a lot of money. Yet I am thankful that my father did not insulate me from the painful financial results of those decisions. Experience is a wonderful teacher.

Chapter 11

PRACTICAL POINTERS

Advertisements

America is the most marketed-to culture in history. We are constantly confronted by powerful pictures and advertisements designed to persuade us to spend money. To survive, you will need to forearm yourself and understand how advertisements work. The purpose of an advertisement is to move you as quickly as possible from where you are to where the marketer wants you. Remember, this may not be where *you* want to go.

Marketers know that if you take time to consider whether you really need their product, you may back off. This is why you often see signs announcing that a sale is "One Day Only" or a "Limited Time Offer." The intent of such advertising is to keep you from stopping and considering before you buy.

Understand that when you walk into a store, you are entering a battlefield. You are trying to purchase only what you need, and the seller is trying to persuade you to spend more than you planned. To accomplish this, advertisements are skillfully designed to lengthen your list of "needs."

A Real Bargain?

It is important to understand that 50% off is not always a bargain. It is easy to get pulled in by sales and huge discounts, but if the item is not something you need, you are paying too much regardless of how low the price is. As a young man, I bought a desk at an auction simply because I thought it was cheap. Actually, it was expensive

because I didn't need it. Be careful at auctions! People bring things home from auctions that they had never before considered buying, but the price was so low they couldn't resist.

Shop with a List

One way to combat the pressure of advertisements is to always shop with a list. Before you leave home, list the items you need. Then stick with your list and check off the items as you shop. This will help you avoid buying impulsively and arriving home with unneeded items.

Write Out Your Vision for Your Family

You will find it much easier to agree with your spouse and family on daily purchases if you first unite on your vision and the direction you want to go. This will take prayer and good communication as a husband and wife. Do you want to live debt-free, share more with others, and teach your children to focus their lives on the Kingdom of God? If you can unite on a vision like this, it will be easier to agree on whether or not to take that expensive vacation or continually spend money on eating out. Many couples have found value in writing out their vision. I encourage you to do this.

Communicate the Vision

Once you have a Kingdom vision for your family, be sure to communicate it to your children. They need to hear you talk about your vision. Over time, your goals will tend to become theirs. It will be easier for you to convince them they don't really need that new toy or gadget if they know you are trying to share as much as possible with others. Use your devotional times to point out Bible verses that support your vision. Read stories of struggles in other parts of the world. This will help your children gain a picture of what really matters and provide clear pointers to the direction your family is going.

Develop an Eternal Value System

Jesus said, "For what shall it profit a man, if he shall gain the whole world, and lose his own soul?"[1] Some things are more important than others, and the only earthly things with eternal value are the souls of people. It

> *The true value of everything is determined in eternity.*

---

[1] Mark 8:36

is possible to become so focused on money and possessions that we neglect things of greater value.

God wants us, as stewards, to give thoughtful care to our use of material things. However, we must never forget that the true value of everything is determined in eternity. Regardless of how much emphasis your culture or community puts on material wealth, the eternal destiny of souls will always be more important than dollars.

Bible Verses Regarding Money & Possessions

The Overriding Purpose of Life and Labor

Matthew 25:31–46

Acts 20:33–35

Galatians 6:10

Ephesians 4:28

1 Timothy 6:17–19

Importance of Diligence and Faithfulness

Proverbs 6:6–8

Proverbs 24:33, 34

Proverbs 27:23–27

Matthew 25:14–30

1 Thessalonians 4:11, 12

2 Thessalonians 3:10–12

1 Timothy 5:8

Importance of Trusting God for the Future

Psalm 84:12

Proverbs 11:28

Matthew 6:25–34

Mark 4:18, 19

Luke 12:22–32

Philippians 4:6

The Need for Contentment

Psalm 37:16

Proverbs 30:8, 9
Luke 12:13–15
Philippians 4:11–13
1 Timothy 6:6–8
Hebrews 13:5

Warnings Against Accumulating Wealth

Proverbs 23:4, 5
Proverbs 28:20
Matthew 6:19–24
Luke 6:24
Luke 12:13–21
1 Timothy 6:9, 10

Dealing with Debt

Psalm 37:21
Proverbs 3:27, 28
Proverbs 22:7
Ecclesiastes 5:5
Luke 6:34, 35
Romans 13:7, 8

Giving

Matthew 6:1–4
Mark 14:3–9
Luke 12:33, 34
1 Corinthians 16:2
2 Corinthians 8:1–16
2 Corinthians 9:6, 7
Galatians 6:10
1 Timothy 6:17–19

ABOUT THE AUTHOR

Gary Miller was raised in an Anabaptist community in California and today lives with his wife Patty and family in the Pacific Northwest. Gary's enthusiasm for Kingdom building has prompted him to write the Kingdom-Focused Living series. He also continues to write teaching manuals for use in the SALT Microfinance program in developing countries. See pages 69–71 for a list of his published works.

Have you been inspired by Gary's materials? Maybe you have questions? Perhaps you even disagree with the author. Share your thoughts by sending an e-mail to kingdomfinance@camoh.org or writing to Christian Aid Ministries, P.O. Box 360, Berlin, Ohio 44610.

ADDITIONAL RESOURCES

by Gary Miller

KINGDOM-FOCUSED LIVING SERIES

Kingdom-Focused Finances for the Family
This first book in the Kingdom-Focused Living series is realistic, humorous, and serious about getting us to become stewards instead of owners. *240 pages*

Charting a Course in Your Youth
A serious call to youth to examine their faith, focus, and finances. *211 pages*

Going Till You're Gone
A plea for godly examples—for older men and women who will demonstrate a Kingdom-focused vision all the way to the finish line. *281 pages*

The Other Side of the Wall
Biblical principles that apply to all Christians who want to reflect God's heart in giving, whether by meeting financial needs in their local community or by seeking to alleviate poverty abroad. *250 pages*

Budgeting Made Simple

A budgeting workbook in a ring binder; complements *Kingdom-Focused Finances for the Family*.

Small Business Handbook

A manual used in microfinance programs in Third World countries. Includes devotionals and practical business teaching. Ideal for missions and churches. *136 pages*

AUDIO AND POWER POINT SEMINARS

Kingdom-Focused Finances Seminar—3 audio CDs

This three-session seminar takes you beyond our culture's view of money and possessions, and challenges you to examine your heart by looking at your treasure.

Kingdom-Focused Finances Seminar Audio PowerPoint—3 CDs

With the visual aid included on these CDs, you can now follow along on the slides Gary uses in his seminars while you listen to the presentation. A good tool for group study or individual use. A computer is needed to view these CDs.

AUDIO BOOKS, NARRATED BY THE AUTHOR

Kingdom-Focused Finances for the Family, Charting a Course in Your Youth, Going Till You're Gone, and *The Other Side of the Wall.*

Christian Aid Ministries

Christian Aid Ministries was founded in 1981 as a nonprofit, tax-exempt 501(c)(3) organization. Its primary purpose is to provide a trustworthy and efficient channel for Amish, Mennonite, and other conservative Anabaptist groups and individuals to minister to physical and spiritual needs around the world. This is in response to the command ". . . do good unto all men, especially unto them who are of the household of faith" (Galatians 6:10).

Each year, CAM supporters provide approximately 15 million pounds of food, clothing, medicines, seeds, Bibles, Bible story books, and other Christian literature for needy people. Most of the aid goes to orphans and Christian families. Supporters' funds also help clean up and rebuild for natural disaster victims, put up Gospel billboards in the U.S., support several church-planting efforts, operate two medical clinics, and provide resources for needy families to make their own living. CAM's main purposes for providing aid are to help and encourage God's people and bring the Gospel to a lost and dying world.

CAM has staff, warehouse, and distribution

networks in Romania, Moldova, Ukraine, Haiti, Nicaragua, Liberia, and Israel. Aside from management, supervisory personnel, and bookkeeping operations, volunteers do most of the work at CAM locations. Each year, volunteers at our warehouses, field bases, DRS projects, and other locations donate over 200,000 hours of work.

CAM's ultimate purpose is to glorify God and help enlarge His kingdom. ". . . whatsoever ye do, do all to the glory of God" (1 Corinthians 10:31).

THE WAY TO GOD AND PEACE

We live in a world contaminated by sin. Sin is anything that goes against God's holy standards. When we do not follow the guidelines that God our Creator gave us, we are guilty of sin. Sin separates us from God, the source of life.

Since the time when the first man and woman, Adam and Eve, sinned in the Garden of Eden, sin has been universal. The Bible says that we all have "sinned and come short of the glory of God" (Romans 3:23). It also says that the natural consequence for that sin is eternal death, or punishment in an eternal hell: "Then when lust hath conceived, it bringeth forth sin: and sin, when it is finished, bringeth forth death" (James 1:15).

But we do not have to suffer eternal death in hell. God provided forgiveness for our sins through the death of His only Son, Jesus Christ. Because Jesus was perfect and without sin, He could die in our place. "For God so loved the world that he gave his only begotten Son, that whosoever believeth in him should not perish, but have everlasting life" (John 3:16).

A sacrifice is something given to benefit someone

else. It costs the giver greatly. Jesus was God's sacrifice. Jesus' death takes away the penalty of sin for everyone who accepts this sacrifice and truly repents of their sins. To repent of sins means to be truly sorry for and turn away from the things we have done that have violated God's standards. (Acts 2:38; 3:19).

Jesus died, but He did not remain dead. After three days, God's Spirit miraculously raised Him to life again. God's Spirit does something similar in us. When we receive Jesus as our sacrifice and repent of our sins, our hearts are changed. We become spiritually alive! We develop new desires and attitudes (2 Corinthians 5:17). We begin to make choices that please God (1 John 3:9). If we do fail and commit sins, we can ask God for forgiveness. "If we confess our sins, he is faithful and just to forgive us our sins, and to cleanse us from all unrighteousness" (1 John 1:9).

Once our hearts have been changed, we want to continue growing spiritually. We will be happy to let Jesus be the Master of our lives and will want to become more like Him. To do this, we must meditate on God's Word and commune with God in prayer. We will testify to others of this change by being baptized and sharing the good news of God's victory over sin and death. Fellowship with a faithful group of believers will strengthen our walk with God (1 John 1:7).